Valley Experiences

And The Blessings That Follow

Norma Elizabeth Glaze
&
Written by my niece, Dr. Victoria Haddad

Dedication

This book is dedicated to all of God's wonderful people. To my mother "Mavis Elaine Spence Bennett Ferguson" who passed away in 2005. My six amazing children (Roy, Veronica, Wayne, Anthony, Sandra, and Pete). My older sister "Sylvia," and my two brothers "Sylvester" and "Hugh."

I am also dedicating my book to my grandchildren, nieces, nephews, cousins, and everyone reading this book.

Table of Contents

Prefix

I am reaching out with the hope that my story will resonates with ladies who are currently navigating the valleys of life. I am encouraging them to lift their voices in praise to God, even amidst the unpredictability and difficulties they maybe facing.

Life, as we know, can present us with an array of challenges. Some of which can feel insurmountable.

It is during these particularly trying times that our faith is put to the most rigorous tests.

No matter the struggles you are going through; whether it is the pain of abuse or the anxiety that comes from strained relationships and the overwhelming sense of despair that life sometimes bring.

The blessing and comfort of the Lord are always within reach.

I am speaking from experience and have traversed a difficult path that felt at times as if it would consume me.

There were moments in my life when the weight of my circumstances felt unbearably heavy.

Particularly during periods when I felt unloved and unwanted by my father. Neglect and abuse by my husband within our marriage, which compounded my feelings of worthlessness.

I have experienced near-death situations that seemed hopeless, and I have endured the heartbreaking reality of losing everything I owned—over and over again.

Yet, what stands out to me through these trials is that God never turned His back on me.

During my lowest points, in the moments that seemed the darkest, He was there, guiding me through my pain.

In His perfect timing and through His immense grace, I transformed from a hurting and broken woman into a vessel filled with His love.

Today, I stand as a testimony of His incredible power and unconditional love.

I feel compelled to reach out to others who are in similar situations, urging them to cling to hope and not lose faith in God, no matter how bleak their circumstances may appear.

The Bible reminds us to worship God not only in times of joy but also during trials. Worshiping Him amid adversity is an act of faith; it is our way of acknowledging his sovereignty and recognizing His present.

Psalm 34:1 encourages us with the exhortation to "Bless the Lord at all times; for His praise shall continually be in our mouths." This directive serves as a reminder that our praises can bring light even into our darkest hours.

The Lord invites us to place our trust in Him, even when life feels like an insurmountable challenge. With His unwavering support, we can rise above our valley experiences and find strength.

This book is written from my steadfast belief in God's transformative power; He is greater than any challenge we may face in life.

Throughout the pages of the Bible, we can find numerous examples of individuals who triumphed over adversity. Consider Paul and Silas; in Acts 16:25-26, they boldly prayed and sang praises at midnight despite being imprisoned unjustly.

Their unwavering faith led to a miraculous earthquake that shook the very foundations of their prison, breaking their chains and ultimately leading them to their freedom.

Similarly, the story of Job stands out as a powerful testament of enduring faith. In his life, he faced unimaginable losses. His wealth, children, and health were stripped away. But rather than cursing God, he chose to worship the Lord, and demonstrate his unwavering faith as he proclaimed, "The Lord gave, and the Lord taken away; but blessed be the name of the Lord" (Job 1:21).

It is entirely natural for our difficulties and unexpected situations to lead us to question God's intentions and presence in our lives. However, we must not lose sight of the truth encapsulated in Romans 8:18, which reminds us that "the sufferings of this present time are not worthy to be compared with the glory that is to be revealed to us."

In the midst of your challenges, know this: you are not alone. God sees your pain, knows your heartbreak, and He deeply cares for you.

Together, with His grace as our anchor, we can navigate these valleys and emerge stronger. God want us to be filled with hope because of His renewed purpose for our lives.

Chapter 1

My name is Norma Elizabeth Bennett-Glaze, and this is my story. I was born on the island of Jamaica, in a small town known as "Springfield" in the parish of St. James – located in Montego Bay.

My father 'Harold Bennett' was the Pastor of one of the smaller Pentecostal-Apostolic churches in our city, a man admired for his unwavering faith and kindness, but he was also a talented suit maker, known for his craftsmanship and attention to detail.

His warm smile and encouraging words drew people to him, but he was adopted as a baby by "the Bennett family."

My mother "Mavis Bennett Ferguson" was the heart of our family, a devoted and loving mother who dedicated her life to being a stay-at-home mother and the supportive pastor's wife.

With a spirit nurturing as a gardener tending to a struggling vineyard, she worked tirelessly to keep our family united.

Her own childhood was marred by tragedy; she lost her parents at a very young age and was raised by her aunt with financial difficulties.

Yet, despite these struggles, she radiated with grace, teaching us the values of kindness and compassion in the face of adversity.

Together, my parents welcome six children— four boys and two girls into the world. However, our family was marked by heartbreak, as one of my siblings was stillborn, leaving an indescribable void in our hearts.

This loss was a heavy burden that added to the complexity of our family drama.

My oldest sister is "Sylvia," my oldest brother "Ronald," followed by my second oldest brother "Sylvester," then I, followed by my youngest brother "Hugh."

Our struggles began at my tender age of five when the delicate fabric of our family started to unravel.

My parents' separation was a fierce storm that I could not fully understand, leaving me engulfed in an overwhelming sadness and an aching longing for the innocence of happier times.

My father took my three oldest siblings with him, leaving my younger brother Hugh and me in the care of our mother.

Despite their roles as leaders within our church community, my parents faced a tumultuous period in their marriage, riddled with deep-seated challenges.

Financial difficulties loomed over our household, exacerbating tensions and leading to arguments that became a constant, sorrowful backdrop of our childhood.

As the years rolled by, the weight of their struggles grew more oppressive, kindling a sense of despair that culminated in the eventual shattering of their union.

In a moment that seemed to sever the already fraying bonds of our family, my father fell in love with another church member.

He chose to abandon his responsibilities; not only to his wife but also to me and Hugh. Pursuing a new life filled with promises and dreams he had seemingly forgotten us.

He started a new family, welcoming more children into the world, deepening the wound left in our hearts.

For Hugh and me, grappling with the reality of growing up without our father was an incredibly painful journey, marked by confusion and loss.

We were too young to grasp the full implications of our father's departure. All we knew was that our mother seemed frequently sad and often cried. A stark contrast to the warmth and security we once felt.

With his abrupt exit, there was no chance for goodbyes, no opportunity to express our feelings, which compounded our grief.

The years passed, and the absence of my father created a profound ache within us.

I began to perceive the world as a place often devoid of divine intervention, filled with unanswered questions and a longing for guidance. It was only after much time and reflection that I felt God stepping in, gently reassuring me of His promises and love.

Despite the tumultuous environment fostered by my father's absence, there was also an opportunity and invitation to lean deeply into our faith.

In the midst of our turmoil, I learned to lean on God more than ever; I truly thank Him every day for never giving up on us, even when feelings of abandonment surged in waves.

As I saw my mother's struggle with depression and stress. the sense of helplessness sometimes loomed around.

All I ever wanted was to reduce her suffering, to shower her with blessings, and to love her in ways that would ease her pain and rekindle her joy.

Limited by my youth and innocence, I could not do anything. More than hope and pray for brighter days, waiting for the moment when the shadows of our past would finally lift.

Chapter 2

Not long after Dad left, we received the devastating news that our brother Ronald had passed away from pneumonia. The shock came swiftly, and we were unprepared for the emotional turmoil that followed.

Losing him felt like another wrench being forced through our hearts. Each twist pushing us deeper into a dark valley of despair.

Our family bond, already fragile, seemed irreparably frayed.

This tragedy hit Mom particularly hard, worsening her struggles with depression.

In an attempt to console her, I often wrap my arms around her, hoping to absorb the pain she was feeling.

My gestures, however, were not enough to heal the wounds that tragedy had inflicted upon us.

Mom sank into a deep depression, so profound that she suffered a nervous breakdown. The once vibrant mother was now unable to maintain her normal routine.

Our situation worsened to the point where we faced the harsh realities of hunger, and we had nowhere to lay our heads at night.

In a desperate bid to find stability, Mom made the difficult decision to move in with her grandmother. Her parents had passed away when she was just a child, so her grandmother, who was our great-grandmother was consider her mom.

However, this arrangement was not without its challenges. Great-grandma's home was small and crowded, especially since Mom's sister, Aunt Sarah, lived there with her husband and two children.

They had become a part of great-grandma's daily life, and tensions simmered between Aunt Sarah and Mom, creating an uncomfortable atmosphere.

Despite these challenges, we tried to make the best of our situation. However, life continued to throw curveballs at us. One heartbreaking morning, we awoke with hope only to find our that great-grandma had passed away.

The devastating news was shocking, but she passed away peacefully in her sleep. She had been okay when she went to bed, and now, her absence left a void that echoed through our already troubled lives.

Each loss seemed to compound our suffering; life was relentless in its trials. I often found myself wishing desperately for a magic solution. A way to snap my fingers and return things to the way they were before.

With our only place to live now taken, we found ourselves once again without a place to call our own.

In the midst of these trials, Mom's faith in the Lord remained unwavering. Despite the unbearable burdens she was bearing, she chose to trust in God.

She was stepping out in faith. Even though her spirits and strength were draining low.

In our desperation, mom began to explore many opportunities to earn money.

She started crafting and selling straw baskets, but the income was hardly sufficient to keep our empty stomachs filled.

Realizing the basket sales weren't enough, she turned to sewing clothes for people in the community and within the church. However, the struggling economy meant that orders were few and far between.

Finally, in an effort to bring in more money, she began baking assorted goods to sell at school during lunchtime, hoping that this would provide a breakthrough. Yet even this effort fell short as sales were limited, and we often went without food.

We were in desperation and our family's needs felt insurmountable. I watched as my mother's eyes filled with sadness, realizing the weight of her inability to provide for us as she would like to.

My brother and I felt her pain, a raw reminder of the reality we were living in. Every day, we prayed desperately, asking for the basic necessities of food and a stable home.

Despite the overwhelming challenges we were facing, we held steadfast to the fact that our struggles would not dictate our future.

We clung to our faith, by the belief that, through God's grace, we would rise above our circumstances and ultimately live a fulfilling life.

Mom, though physically weakened, remained our anchor. Her love and determination was a source of strength for my brother and me.

She took on multiple roles to provide stability amidst the chaos, doing everything she could to ensure we felt the warmth of her love despite our cold reality.

As she navigated through life difficulties, she often recited the words that became a salve to our troubled hearts: "God said unto us, my grace is sufficient for thee: for my strength is made perfect in weakness. Most gladly therefore will I rather glory in my infirmities, that the power of Christ may rest upon me. Therefore, I take pleasure in infirmities, in reproaches, in necessities, in persecutions, in distresses for Christ's sake: for when I am weak, then am I strong." (2 Corinthians 12:9-10).

Mom acts of faith was clear; she prayed for us, offered encouragement, and reminding us that serving God during desperation will bring great result.

Even when we did not see the immediate results of our prayers, she encouraged us to persist. For the Lord will intervene when He is ready.

Her unwavering faith in God and her unconditional love stayed with us even in our darkest hours.

Author Lisa Wingate once wrote, "Sometimes the darkest trials make way for the brightest dawns."

Indeed, my family and I faced significant challenges, but through courage and an open heart, we grew stronger. Hoping to triumph over our adversities.

Chapter 3

Life took yet another unexpected turn, throwing us into a whirlwind of challenges. As we made our way down the winding path into the depths of our valley, it felt as though hope was dimming with each step, constricting our spirits and making it hard to see any glimmer of improvement on the horizon.

During this dark period, my mother's confrontation with the harsh realities of life intensified, and the warmth of ordinary sunshine transformed into a mere shadow of a memory from happier days.

Amidst this growing despair, my mother faced an agonizing choice. One I never foreseen coming.

A decision that would fundamentally alter the course of my life, she resolved to place me for adoption with one of my elementary school teachers.

This teacher, a kind and compassionate woman who had closely observed the struggles of our family was endearing and extended her hand with an offer that seemed almost unbelievable.

She and her husband, after many years of marriage, found themselves childless and longing for a family of their own.

When they approached my mother regarding the possibility of adoption, she ultimately consented, firmly believing that I would have a better chance of a happy and stable life with them than she could ever provide under our circumstances.

In that moment, my heart plummeted. Confusion and dread flooded my senses; I had already experienced the wrenching loss of my father, and the thought of losing my mother was unbearable, regardless of how dismal our situation had become.

The bonds of family felt sacred, to me irreplaceable. I clung to the hope that no matter how challenging things got. I needed my family, my mother, my siblings, and particularly my younger brother, Hugh.

Upon moving in with my new adoptive parents, I found myself nestled in the care of a couple that many children would be fortunate to call their own.

They embraced me with warmth and kindness, determined to provide everything I could possibly need. Their home was a sprawling haven, filled with light and laughter, set on several acres of fertile land adorned with flourishing fruit trees.

For the first time, I had my own room. A newfound luxury that seemed almost surreal. My adoptive parents were not just financially stable; they radiated warmth and generosity, always ensuring that I never went hungry.

Their meals were plentiful, a sharp contrast to the gnawing hunger I had known for so long. We danced and sang together, sharing precious moments that felt like distant dreams from the harsh reality I had left behind.

Yet, despite the abundance of love and stability enveloping me, I was haunted by a profound emptiness. I felt adrift in a sea of unfamiliarity, yearning for the connection to my true family.

My new parents, despite their best efforts to create a nurturing environment; I felt distant. I found myself missing the nuances of my mother's soothing voice, the infectious laughter of my siblings, and especially the unique bond I shared with Hugh.

No amount of material wealth or affection from my adoptive parents seemed capable of filling the aching void in my heart.

Simultaneously, my mother was navigating her own tumultuous journey. The burden of losing me weighed heavily on her spirit, and she grappled daily with her sense of loss.

Even amidst her pain, she forged ahead, determined to rise from her difficult circumstances. Miraculously, two years later, things began to take a turn for the better.

Although the road ahead was still fraught with challenges, she managed to secure a job, which allowed her to rent a modest two-bedroom apartment.

It may have been old and worn, but to my mother, it felt like a substantial blessing. One that provided newfound stability and hope in a life that had been too often marred by uncertainty.

One fateful day, my mother bravely reached out to my adoptive parents to discuss the possibility of bringing me back home.

The couple was taken aback by her request, but deep down, they recognized the undeniable truth: I was yearning for my mother and the life we had once shared.

With heavy hearts and after much deliberation, they made the gut-wrenching decision to let me go, fully aware that my happiness lay in reuniting with my family.

When I returned to my mother's side, an indescribable wave of joy washed over me. In that moment, I felt as if all my prayers had been answered.

My mother welcomed me with open arms, her heart no longer encumbered by memories of my father, radiating happiness with each visit from my sister Sylvia and brother Sylvester.

Our family began to feel whole again in that small apartment, and I treasured every moment spent together, relishing the simple yet profound joys of being reunited.

However, just as we began to find our rhythm and reclaim a sense of normalcy, tragedy struck once more.

My mother suffered another nervous breakdown, throwing our family into disarray.

It felt as though we had been yanked back into a cycle of anguish, facing yet another overwhelming challenge that loomed over us like a dark cloud.

The emotional weight we carried was suffocating, filled with anxiety and despair as we grappled with uncertainty.

In the wake of this breakdown, my mother was left utterly shattered, wrestling with an acute sense of exhaustion and despair that seemed insurmountable.

Yet, even in her deepest moments of darkness, she clung tenaciously to her faith, seeking solace and strength from God.

Questions haunted her thoughts—why did we have to endure such relentless trials, and when would relief grace our lives once more?

It is essential to recognize that experiencing a nervous breakdown does not imply a failure in one's spiritual journey. Instead, it serves as a poignant reminder that during our darkest moments, we can turn to God for solace and strength.

Just as the prophet Elijah found himself wandering in despair, wishing for an end to his life in the wilderness, we too can feel overwhelmed by our burdens. However, God responded to Elijah not with condemnation but with compassion, providing rest, nourishment, and a reminder that he was not alone.

As I navigated the complexities of our struggles, I understood the importance of maintaining faith and trust in God, even amidst our darkest trials.

The scripture reassured us that "The Lord is nigh unto them that are of a broken heart; and save such as be of a contrite spirit. Many are the afflictions of the righteous: but the LORD deliver him out of them all."

In this journey together, the belief that we were not alone became our beacon of hope, guiding us through the shadows of our trials.

Chapter 4

By the time I was thirteen years old; things had taken another turn. Mom had a nervous breakdown and could no longer take care of us. Because of my young age, I did not understand much at the time, but I thank God for revealing to me throughout life's difficulties that spiritual strength is essential.

We wanted to protect Mom's mental health and keep her safe from the things that were overwhelming her, but it was hard for us to focus only on what truly mattered and let go of unnecessary stress when our lives were filled with it.

Mom's nervous breakdown made it feel like her life was derailing, yet she did not let go of God.

Romans 8:28 reminded us that "All things work together for good to them that love God and to them who are the called according to His purpose."

Even in Mom's pain, God was working, bringing healing and comfort into her life.

Mom did not give up on God. She believed that serving the Lord during her nervous breakdown was not about ignoring her struggles but about completely surrendering to Him.

She trusted that God was with her, even when life seemed overwhelming.

During services, she prayed, sought support, and took steps toward healing each day.

She continued to serve God in ways that reflected His grace and love for her children.

Mom's journey through this challenging season was a powerful testimony of God's faithfulness. She believed that God would carry us through difficult moments.

However, our life struggles were worsening each day, and once again, Mom thought that sending me to live with a new foster mother would be the best possibility for me.

This woman was a church member and someone Mom became friend with after meeting her at church.

Mom thought that sending me to live with this church member was a great idea, as she would see us at church weekly and visit me regularly.

But this foster mother had two sides. One side was the good side she showed everyone in church, where she appeared nice and friendly. Someone everyone loved.

However, I got to see the other side, the side that no one else saw. It was the cruel side that beat me severely every day and forced me to work like a slave. She asked me to clean the entire house on my own daily.

Paul faced tremendous hardships, including imprisonment, physical pain, and emotional struggles.

Yet, he declared, "I can do all this through Him who gives me strength" (Philippians 4:13).

These examples reminded me that God will not abandon me in my weakness. Instead, He will draw me closer and offer me comfort and strength.

This foster mom had me cooking daily meals and baking assortment of cookies and cakes to sell in the market on weekends.

She never sent me to school and kept me at home, forcing me to work throughout each day.

At first glance, this woman seemed like the best mom a child could ask for, but she was the meanest person I ever met.

When Mom visited, this foster mother would be so nice to me in front of her. I was not allowed to be alone with Mom, so I could not tell her what was really going on. If I tried, I would be beaten severely after Mom left.

Every day, I cried out to God, begging Him to take away the pain and help me either return home to be with my mom or go back to live with the first couple I had been with.

On one of my mom's visits, a neighbor told her that they suspected I was being abused and that she should remove me from that home.

I was so grateful to God for revealing the situation to the neighbor.

My mom fearful of confronting my foster mother by herself since she was visiting alone. So, she went back home and sent my sister Sylvia to come and get me.

Sylvia and my older brother Sylvester had recently moved back home and were now living with Mom, since my father had decided to move to London, UK, with his new family.

Sylvia was not a shy person and was not afraid of the woman. She was happy to come and get me so we could be a family again.

I was overjoyed when Sylvia showed up for me. I thanked God for remembering me and for bringing us back together as a family.

I remembered the story of Moses and understood how he felt when he "chose rather to suffer affliction with the people of God than to enjoy the pleasures of sin for a season" (Hebrews 11:25).

I rather suffer with my family than live in foster homes.

Even though we all knew that if it was not for God's help, I would not have made it back home safely.

I always wished I was able to spend more time with my dad, even though I felt like his departure changed our lives forever.

I always wished Dad the best of luck from that day on and prayed that his decision to move to London, UK, with his new family was the happiest moment of his life.

He visited us many years later and reassured us of his love, but he passed away when he was in his sixties.

I always wished he had made the decision to stay with us.

Chapter 5

My mom continued to attend church week after week, even though she was facing series of painful situations that seemed relentless. She was a truly beautiful woman, yet the struggles of her life often overshadowed that beauty.

Nevertheless, her faith in the Lord remained unwavering. Mom understood that the only one who could provide her with the help she so desperately needed was God, and she clung to Him with all her heart and soul.

In many ways, she reminded me of Job, whose faith remained resolute even in the face of unimaginable trials.

Like Job, mom often express her steadfast trust in the Lord, echoing the words: "Though he slays me, yet will I trust in him: but I will maintain mine own ways before him." (Job 13:15).

Mom strength was always inspirational, but for my siblings and me, our relationship with God was not as deep. As children, we were eager to find a different path, one that often led us away from the teachings of the Lord.

As a teenager, I met a young man who was charming, handsome, and just a couple of years older than me.

He seemed to embody everything I was searching for in a relationship. A perfect prince to rescue me from my struggles.

But, as I would soon learn, appearances can be deceptive.

Before long, I found myself pregnant with our first son, Roy, and I was forced to drop out of high school just shy of graduation.

The young man I had fallen for showed little interest in taking on the responsibilities of fatherhood and was quick to abandon me as if I were a used napkin, tossed aside without a second thought.

In that moment of despair, I felt a surge of divine intervention as God stepped in on my behalf, offering me solace.

As I navigated the harsh realities of early parenthood, I found myself grappling with a vast array of challenges. The fears about the future, insecurities stemming from my youth, and a desperate longing for the love I thought I would receive from the man I had fallen for.

The dreams of building a life together were vanishing and leaving me disappointed.

These experiences were, indeed, tumultuous, but it was providing me fertile ground for my personal growth.

The relationship that I had cherished with my first love began to deteriorate as we both confronted the new responsibilities that parenthood foisted upon us.

We often fell short, struggling to maintain a healthy relationship while trying to care for our child.

There is no love quite like that of a parent for their child, a bond that bestows a unique sense of purpose.

Though my experience of teenage parenthood was riddled with trials, it also presented me the opportunity to redefine my aspirations and goals, enabling growth that I never anticipated.

Our son became our great motivation, pushing us to work tirelessly to achieve our dreams and build a better future for both of us.

Throughout this journey, I continually reminded myself that my circumstances did not define my worth or potential.

I was profoundly grateful to God for introducing me to the mother of the man I was in love with. This lady was like a mother-in-law to me. She quickly became my confidante and a maternal figure in my life.

Taking charge of the situation, she insisted that her son step up to fulfill his responsibilities as a father. Her support meant the world to me.

She even invited me to move in with her and the love of my life – her son. For he was still living with her.

Her compassion lifted my spirits during a time when I felt lost and overwhelmed.

My mother was enduring her own struggles with both illness and financial instability. She also moved in with one of the church sisters – another friend from the church.

Though it was heartbreaking to see her suffer, knowing she was in a safe environment brought me a sense of relief.

My mother-in-law was a remarkable woman. As she took me under her wing, treating me as if I were her own daughter during my pregnancy – make me feel like the best decision.

She skillfully managed her own large family but never made me feel like a burden. Instead, she showered me with love and support, which I cherished profoundly.

Through it all, I learned to believe in myself and to trust in my ability to navigate the challenges of motherhood.

Despite the countless obstacles I faced with my first son. I also experienced moments of immense joy, love, and pride.

My relationship began to steadily improved; we shared moments of happiness that occasionally outweighed the difficulties.

Watching our first child grow and thrive, filled with the love and care we were striving to provide, became one of the most rewarding experiences of my life.

Though he was not the first grandchild for my mother-in-law, she accepted Roy with open arms and loved him as if he were her own.

Her dedication to our family was a blessing, one I remain thankful for every day.

This journey, though challenging, shaped me into the person I am today, and I carry with me the lessons of resilience, faith, and the profound power of love.

Chapter 6

At such remarkably young age, I found myself stepping into a world that most people my young age were not yet prepared to navigate. My relationship with my husband has taken a promising turn, blossoming as we welcomed more children into our lives and built a more solid foundation together.

Our journey began with the birth of our son, Roy, who quickly became a big brother when our daughter, Veronica, joined the family. Soon after, Wayne arrived, each child marking a milestone in our lives just a few years apart.

As we embraced parenthood, we were not only discovering our identities but also learning to forge a life together, overcoming challenges that tested our resilience and deepened our faith with one another.

We made the significant decision to marry at a young age, unwittingly weaving our lives into a complex tapestry of responsibility and personal growth. Initially, what started as a friendship gradually transformed into a profound relationship filled with uncharted territory.

However, marrying early came with its own set of trials. We faced countless financial struggles, the daunting responsibilities of raising young children, and the challenge of carving out quality time for each other amidst the chaos.

It was never a smooth sail; we often found ourselves challenged not just by external pressures but also by our own shortcomings.

Our communication was far from ideal, and at times, immaturity crept into our relationship, amplifying our misunderstandings.

Fortunately, my husband's mother played a crucial role as a steadfast support, deeply committed to our growth as a couple.

As the years passed and our family expanded, we welcomed even more children into our lives: Anthony and Sandra came along, making them our fourth and fifth children.

By the time I reached my mid-twenties, I was the parent of five beautiful children, each of whom imparted unique lessons about patience, adaptability, and the ability to savor joy in the smallest of moments.

In those early years, the weight of responsibility often felt suffocating. My husband and I were still learning the ropes of effective communication, and our emotions often ran high.

The societal pressure to "have it all together" sometimes left us questioning whether we had taken on too much too soon.

Yet, with every obstacle we encountered, we saw an opportunity to learn and grow together.

During these years, disagreements became more frequent, and we often lost sight of solutions that could work for both of us.

Exhaustion tested our patience as we navigated the sleepless nights filled with our children's cries and the relentless tantrums that often felt never-ending.

Emotionally, we were both evolving in ways that often felt out of our control.

My husband began growing into a man who could embody both strength and vulnerability, but he struggled to admit when he felt overwhelmed or to rise to the occasion when it mattered most.

This dynamic seeped into our daily lives, creating a ripple effect that affected our relationship and our children.

Despite the strains, I tried to remain empathetic, striving to see the world through the eyes of our kids.

Each struggle presented me with a deeper appreciation for the effort and love needed to build a family.

There were moments when we learned to celebrate the small victories, but there were times when I felt an unsettling sense of doubt about his commitment to me.

At times, he was letting those doubts distance us from each other, which in turn affected our children.

Through these experiences, we came to realize that growth isn't defined by perfection but is rooted in the commitment to show up each day and do our best, particularly when the going gets tough.

Some of the challenges we faced felt like they were breaking us apart. However, my husband's mother taught him the invaluable lesson that love transcends mere feelings. She told him that love is a conscious choice we must make every day, a pact to grow and evolve together.

We knew we needed to regain our footing in terms of effective communication and prioritize our relationship amidst the tumult of our daily lives.

Each argument, each reconciliation, and every shared moment of laughter was slowly reminding me of our strength as a couple.

As our relationship extended, my husband was getting more abusive towards me, but I was hoping for improvement.

Chapter 7

During those those pivotal years, my husband's mother—who was my best friend took a brave step and traveled to America. She left us behind with the intension of doing all she could to bring us to America as well.

In her new home, she blossomed into a remarkable community member, dedicating herself to vigorous work in New York.

Thanks to her unwavering commitment, she was able to purchase a beautiful home, a space full of hope and potential for her family.

A few years later, she took the significant step of filing for permanent residency for all of her children, an act that opened the door for a new chapter in our lives.

When my husband and I received the heartfelt invitation to come to America, we were overwhelmed with gratitude. It felt like an opportunity to profoundly change the trajectory of our lives and make this land our new home.

However, this new beginning came with heart-wrenching sacrifices. We made the painful decision to leave our children in the care of my mother for a few years until we could purchase a house and apply for their visas.

Leaving my children behind was not merely a decision; it was a moment steeped in emotional complexity. While it was undoubtedly difficult, the decision to leave everything familiar behind was not the hardest choice we faced.

My mother was rising as a person, finding strength and purpose in her church and daily life. She was now working and renting a home that was accommodating to our children.

Our leap of faith was motivated by the hope for a brighter future for our family. A chance to build something new, not only for ourselves, but, more importantly, for our children.

Back home, life was predictable but full of restrictions. We toiled day and night, yet opportunities seemed limited. I often envisioned a better future for my children, one characterized by quality education, safer surrounding environments, and the freedom to dream without barriers.

I believed that America held the promise of realizing those dreams.

The journey to our new home was as emotional as it was physical. Saying goodbye to my children and my mother was a temporary separation, yet it was undeniably heartbreaking.

They have always been our support system, sharing in our joys and sorrows. Despite the deep sorrow in our hearts, we knew we must be courageous for the sake of our children. The future we envisioned needed it.

As we stepped off the plane in America, we were introduced by a whirlwind of emotions and exhausted from the long journey. Yet our hearts were fill with nervous excitement.

The moment felt surreal, as we entered a world that was dazzlingly different from what we had known.

With just a few suitcases and an unshakeable faith, we believed that with God's guidance, we could pave a way for a better life for our family.

The initial days in America were fraught with challenges that tested our resolve and determination.

Every aspect of my life felt uncertain, and adapting to a new culture was daunting.

We budgeted every penny, always keeping our sight set on bringing our children over. At that point, I was not particularly spiritually strong, and my husband had never been a member of the church, but I clung to the belief that prayers were our anchor.

I tried earnestly to pray each night, seeking strength and perseverance amidst the struggles within our marriage.

Everywhere I turned, stories of abuse and difficult relationships circulated. Yet, I found myself grappling with the realities of my own relationship, not fully comprehending how complicated it would become.

Despite the complexities, my husband and I took on several jobs and worked diligently.

Each day, we returned home exhausted, knowing that every dollar we earned will bring us one step closer to fulfilling our dreams.

Yet, even as we fought through challenges, my relationship with my husband began to deteriorate.

While he showed strength in some areas, our physical connection was diminishing.

I pushed myself beyond my comfort zone, learning and adapting to this unfamiliar landscape, while desperately seeking my place within it.

There were days when I felt utterly lost, especially as my husband's sporadic support seemed to fade.

As we navigated, it became increasingly hard for us to lean on each other.

My husband was drifting away, not becoming the personal strength I had hoped for.

Coming to America was supposed to signify a journey of hope and I was hoping that leaving behind our problems, we could improve our marriage and embrace the unknown together.

As we ventured, I was envisioning not only a new home but also a novel version of ourselves.

Settling in America was a testament to my hope for a brighter future for myself and my children. While the sacrifices we made were heavy, they embodied our determination to provide the best possible life for our family.

America stood for a land of opportunity, where we could dream big and pursue our passions. I held fast to the belief that with hard work and perseverance, we would achieve incredible things.

Yet, as the days turned into months, I realized I was mistaken. My relationship with my husband was deteriorating faster than I could have imagined, and the emotional toll it inflicted on me was becoming severe.

I found myself trapped in an abusive situation, feeling powerless as I struggled to keep my family together, all while trying to bring my mom and children to America.

In those moments, the weight of my choices bore heavily on my heart.

Chapter 8

While working hard to bring my family over, I received the unexpected news that I was pregnant with our sixth child "Pete." His arrival marked a significant turning point for us, as he became our last son and the final addition to our family.

With Pete's birth, we felt a renewed sense of purpose to diligently work toward our dream of buying a house. It was important for us to create a stable home where we could eventually bring our five older children and my mother to live with us.

Throughout this journey, I endured many challenges, particularly dealing with my husband's abusive behavior. Despite the hardships, I stayed focused on what truly mattered: the well-being of my children and the realization of our dreams.

We lived modestly, cutting back on luxuries and making do with what we had. Each dollar saved felt like a small victory in our pursuit of a better life.

I recall late nights spent at the kitchen table, meticulously going over our budget, feeling a combination of pride and unwavering determination as we worked toward our goals.

After years of hard work and sacrifices, we finally found the house that felt like home. It wasn't extravagant, but it was perfect for our family's needs.

I vividly remember standing in the empty living room, tears of joy streaming down my face as I envisioned the life we would build together within those walls.

It was far more than just a house; it represented the culmination of countless prayers, sacrifices, and our relentless determination to overcome adversity.

The day we signed the papers and held the keys in our hands stands out as one of the proudest moments of our lives. Purchasing our first home became more than just a financial milestone; it symbolized everything we had triumphed over.

It was a tangible reminder that with faith, hard work, and perseverance, dreams could indeed become reality.

However, while our living situation had improved, my relationship with my husband was deteriorating at an alarming rate.

The abuse had intensified beyond anything I had ever experienced before.

A couple of years after buying our home and reuniting with our children, the cycle of abuse continued unabated.

My husband began dating another woman, often abandoning me and our children to spend time away from home.

There were many times when he would vanish for days on end, lost to a world outside our family.

It was as though he had forgotten he was still married, leaving me to manage everything alone while I juggled the responsibilities of parenting.

I watched helplessly as he started developing a severe addiction to alcohol, escalating his smoking habits as well. His nights were often filled with heavy drinking, returning home inebriated, and unruly.

Each encounter inevitably turning into verbal clashes, filled with cursing and emotional abuse directed not only at me but also towards our oldest sons.

The chaos left me exhausted, and I often went to work feeling drained, having barely slept a wink through the night.

The house became a battleground as he fought, drank, smoked, and broke things in fits of anger.

My children and I lived in constant fear, never knowing what awaited us at the end of each day when I returned home from work.

Their school days were often marred by fatigue, as they too were affected by the tumultuous environment we were living in.

I remember evenings spent with tears streaming down my face, often spilling into my dinner plate as I struggled to eat amidst the emotional turmoil.

Little Pete, our baby, spent many nights with a babysitter who became a vital support system for us.

There were times when I had to ask her to keep him overnight for his safety, knowing it was the only way to ensure he would not be caught up in the chaos of our household.

The babysitter was a remarkable and understanding person whom I could trust. She was providing a small sanctuary for my son during such tumultuous times.

In those darkest hours, my faith and hope became invaluable sources of strength. I immersed myself in prayer, dive deeper into Scripture, and attended church services as a source of comfort and guidance.

One verse that resonated with me deeply was Jeremiah 29:11, "I know the thoughts that I think toward you, saith the Lord, thoughts of peace, and not of evil, to give you an expected end."

God knows the plans He has for us, plans to prosper and not to harm, plans to give us hope and a future.

Holding on to this promise helped me restore some measure of peace and provided assurance that my sacrifices would eventually bear fruit.

As the years unfolded, the reality of my marriage starkly contrasted with the dreams I had once envisioned.

The abuse left me feeling shattered and isolated, yet in the midst of my pain, my steadfast hope was my faith in the Lord.

It was incredibly challenging to keep my faith with the weight of my circumstances pressing down on me.

I found myself crying out to God repeatedly, questioning why I was enduring such suffering and whether He had forgotten about me.

Still, in my bleakest moments, there was a gentle, persistent voice within my heart that whispered, "I am with you." That assurance became my beacon of hope, guiding me through the storm.

Serving the Lord became both my refuge and my driving force. I poured my heart into church activities, finding purpose in volunteering, teaching Sunday school, singing in the choir, and preparing meals for those in need.

These acts of service provided me with a sense of peace and fulfillment that helped distract me from the turbulence of my home life.

Even in the face of my struggles, I found ways to make a positive impact on the lives of others.

My time spent in prayer and reflection became sacred. There were countless nights when I knelt in prayer, laying bare my anguish and pleading for guidance.

The Bible transformed my strength, "Fear not, for I am with you; be not dismayed, for I am your God. I will strengthen you; I will help you; I will uphold you with my righteous right hand" (Isaiah 41:10). In this verse, I found comfort when I felt most vulnerable.

Yet, amidst all this, there were days when the burdens felt nearly insurmountable. Well-meaning words from my husband sometimes compounded my distress.

I made the decision to protect my children and keep moving forward amidst the chaos. Despite it all, I held tightly to the belief that God have a purpose for my life, even if such revelation felt distant.

I learned to cherish joy in small moments, recognizing that even in the depths of despair, there were glimmers of light worth embracing.

Through all the heartache, I stayed resolute in my commitment to find peace, hope, and love for my family and myself.

Chapter 9

My yearning to serve God during the most challenging times fueled my trust in His guidance. It became a commitment to prioritize our well-being, understanding that His desire for us is one of freedom, healing, and restoration.

I vividly remember one evening, coming home with a sense of joy. However, that joy quickly turned to dread as I witnessed my husband react violently when our four-year-old son, Pete, was upset and crying on our way home.

When we got home. In a terrifying moment, my husband grabbed Pete roughly and threw him into the house, causing him to land hard on the floor.

The scream that escaped Pete's lips was heart-wrenching, and in that instant, I knew we needed to find safety away from my husband.

That sense of urgency grew even worse another day when my children expressed their fears. They were home alone and went and hid in a closet, frightened of their father arrival to the house and knocked down their door in a fit of aggression.

I felt powerless and heartbroken as I listened to my daughter call me at work, her voice trembling with fear for their safety. It was clear: we had to find a way out.

With a heavy heart, I called the police, and they arrived promptly, arresting him before any further harm could come to our children.

I was grateful that they were safe that time, and I reached out to a church brother who kindly helped fix the door.

These events were painful for all of us, but I found solace knowing that God was protecting us from being irreparably harmed.

Yet, the danger did not end there. My husband displayed unpredictable and aggressive behavior, and there were moments when I feared for my life. Despite this, I found strength in the most desperate times, pressing on through the struggle.

Even now, I carry the reminders of that fear, particularly when it comes to anything near my neck.

"But thanks be to God, which giveth us the victory through our Lord Jesus Christ." (1 Corinthians 15:57).

I made the heartfelt decision to praise the Lord, who has never failed me. In my prayer and supplication, I cried out to God for a way out of my difficult marriage.

Eventually, I sought a restraining order and filed for divorce, yet he would still find a way to come to our home, breaking windows to get inside.

Despite these attempts to intimidate us, I found solace in knowing that God kept us safe.

One day, overwhelmed with emotion and searching for guidance, I turned to the Bible and read

Isaiah 58. In verse 6, the Lord spoke to my heart: "Is not this the fast that I have chosen? to lose the bands of wickedness, to undo the heavy burdens, and to let the oppressed go free, and that ye break every yoke?" (Isaiah 58:6).

Those words helped me understand that my struggle was not in vain, and that God had a plan for my freedom. I continue to trust in His promises, believing in deliverance and hope for a better future.

Chapter 10

God conversation with me felt as though I was having a personal conversation with a regular person, as if someone were speaking to me face to face. In that moment, I sensed that God was informing me of His intention to release the bindings that held me captive.

Though I was uncertain of how to navigate this daunting situation, God provided clear direction and sent me the support I needed, urging me to seek refuge in a women's shelter.

Following His guidance, I took that pivotal step and reached out to the local abused women's shelter.

They were incredibly understanding and walked me through the process, ultimately welcoming my children and me into a safe space.

It was a tremendous relief to know that we would be in a protected environment.

After several weeks of finding our footing, I knew I needed legal assistance to ensure our safety when we returned home.

I managed to secure a lawyer who helped me obtain a restraining order against my husband, legally prohibiting him from coming near either us or our home.

Yet, despite this protective measure, I still had to contact the police multiple times, as he continued to show up at our house, disregarding the order.

The fear I felt was palpable; when my children spotted him pulling up at the gate, we quickly locked the door.

In these terrifying moments, my children would rush to the attic and hide in the closet, hoping to stay out of sight.

We were gripped with fear, but I found solace in the knowledge that God was keeping us safe.

Each time I called the police, they promptly arrived and instructed him to leave, adding a layer of security in our chaotic lives.

Looking back, it felt like a nightmare, and I was reminded of Psalm 23:4, where David said, "Yea, though I walk through the valley of the shadow of death, I will fear no evil: for God is with me; His rod and staff will comfort me."

God truly was my comforter; without Him, my children and I would not be alive today. He protected us and provided food and shelter during our time of need.

I am a living testimony of the truth that an abusive marriage is contrary to God's intended design for marital relationships.

Marriage, as ordained by God, is meant to be a covenant grounded in love, respect, and mutual submission (Ephesians 5:22-33).

Abuse stands in stark opposition to these sacred principles and is never condoned within the Scriptures.

God is a deity of justice and compassion, one who hears the cries of the poor and the afflicted (Job 34:28).

He calls upon His people to seek safety and restoration, illuminating a path out of darkness.

Serving the Lord amidst difficult circumstances does not equate to enduring abuse in silence. Instead, it involves earnestly seeking His guidance and protection while remaining anchored in faith.

Although my abusive marriage made me feel powerless, I recognized that serving the Lord empowered me to lean on His strength, which is sufficient for every situation.

Through prayer, even when the words seemed difficult to express, I discovered a source of strength that fortified me against daily challenges.

Eventually, I came to understand that serving God does not mean remaining silent or accepting abuse as part of the plan He has laid out for me.

Taking proactive steps to protect myself and my children aligned with God's call for safety and righteousness.

I sought help from trusted pastors, counselors, and domestic violence organizations, understanding that this was a crucial step in reclaiming our lives.

Serving God in this context meant vigilant about our safety and placing my trust in Him to provide the necessary resources and support.

Prayer transformed me into a powerful instrument of faith during my abusive marriage. We prayed for strength and healing, inviting God into our lives and circumstances.

Even amid the turmoil, I prayed for my husband during and after our divorce. The Lord taught me the importance of loving our enemies and praying for those who persecute us, as commanded in Matthew 5:44.

This practice did not excuse his abusive actions, but it placed our situation in God's capable hands, trusting that He would bring about conviction and ultimately change.

Continuing to serve the Lord during such challenging times allowed me to be honest with others about my struggles.

In those moments, I realized that trusting God for my deliverance did not signify passivity. It meant actively seeking His will for my life while acknowledging the painful reality of my circumstances.

Forgiveness emerged as an essential step toward personal healing and liberation, a process that enabled God's peace to fill my heart.

Serving the Lord through forgiveness mirrored His mercy and grace, though it required time, unwavering prayer, and immense support along the way.

I focused on prayer, seeking assistance, and leaning on God's strength to navigate my difficulties.

Through it all, the Lord taught me how to honor Him, even in the midst of profound sadness.

As I navigated the complexities of my abusive marriage, I recognized that serving the Lord was a powerful testimony of His sustaining grace.

It served as a constant reminder that God was always near, even during the heartbreaking experiences I endured within my marriage.

I felt unloved and undervalued in what was meant to be a safe haven.

Trusting others became a challenge when all I could think of was my yearning for my family.

But even in the depths of my suffering, God's love remained steadfast, guiding me through the darkness.

Chapter 11

The strength we need to endure troublesome situations often reveals itself in the most unexpected moments. I remember one day, in particular, when my ex-husband broke down the door and forcibly entered the sanctuary of our home. It was one of the most terrifying experiences of my life.

Despite being divorced, I had been nurturing the hope that we could coexist peacefully, primarily for the sake of our children.

That day, however, shattered the fragile sense of security I had painstakingly rebuilt in the aftermath of our tumultuous separation.

It had started out as an ordinary day, one where I finally felt a semblance of stability returning after the chaos of our divorce.

My small, modest home had transformed into a safe haven and a sacred space filled with laughter, prayer, and healing for both me and my children. I had allowed myself to believe that the worst was behind us.

When I heard the sound of the door being ripped from its hinges, my heart dropped like a stone. An icy wave of fear surged through me as I fully comprehended the situation unfolding before me.

My ex-husband had invaded a space that no longer belonged to him, a place where he had no rights or authority.

For a fleeting moment, I froze, consumed by disbelief and uncertainty.

My thoughts immediately turned to my children, who were playing innocently in another room. I knew that I had to protect them at all costs.

With trembling hands, I dialed for help, feeling both powerless and vulnerable as I did so. In that moment, I also turned inward, praying silently.

I begged God to keep us safe, to grant me the courage I so desperately needed, and to guide me in making the right decisions amidst the oncoming chaos.

As my ex-husband burst through the door, the atmosphere thickened with tension. His anger filled the air, ringing loudly in my ears as he hurled accusations at me with venomous fury, unjustly blaming me for things I had not done.

My children, sensing the danger, huddled close to me, their small bodies trembling in fear as I stood as their shield against the storm of conflict.

That moment tested every ounce of courage I possessed. I took a deep breath, forced myself to remain calm, and spoke firmly, avoiding any escalation of the situation.

I reminded him emphatically that this was no longer his home and that he had no right to trespass on our lives.

My faith in God became my anchor during this tumultuous ordeal. I felt an indescribable strength surging through me, reminding me that I was not alone in this battle.

God stood with me, reinforcing my resolve as I confronted my fear head-on.

Thankfully, help arrived, and my ex-husband was ultimately compelled to leave. As the door slammed shut behind him, a deluge of emotions washed over me—relief, fear, anger, and profound sadness all clamored for attention.

Yet, above all, I felt a deep exhaustion. I was tired of the ceaseless conflict, weary from the gnawing anxiety, and burdened by the weight of all that had transpired.

That night, I prayed like never before, pouring my heart out to God in gratitude for our safety while simultaneously expressing my anger and confusion.

I sought His guidance and wisdom on how to navigate the treacherous path ahead, yearning for the strength to persevere through my struggles.

In the wake of that incident, I took concrete steps to ensure our safety. Changing locks, pursuing legal protections, and seeking the support of friends and family who rallied around us during this frightening time.

Although these actions were challenging, I understood that I had to create a protective environment for my children and myself.

Throughout this ordeal, my faith remained my greatest pillar of strength. I consistently reminded myself that God was my refuge, my protector, and the source of my inner strength.

Even amidst the fear and confusion, I felt His presence guiding me through the dark storm.

This harrowing experience served as a poignant reminder that healing is rarely a linear journey.

Often, the shadows of our past attempt to invade our present, forcing us to confront unresolved fears and emotions.

Nevertheless, through God's unwavering support, I discovered that we can emerge from these trials stronger than we were before.

Reflecting on that moment now, I no longer view it solely as a painful experience; rather, it has become a testament to the stability and resilience that God has instilled in me.

It has helped me recognize that, even when life feels overwhelmingly chaotic, I am never truly alone.

God is my shield, my unwavering protector, and the source of my peace amidst turmoil.

"The Lord is nigh unto them that are of a broken heart; and save such as be of a contrite spirit. Many are the afflictions of the righteous: but the LORD deliver him out of them all." (Psalm 34:18)

Growing up with adversity was no easy feat, but it was a journey that ultimately led us to discover strength and purpose we never knew we had.

In our darkest valleys, God's light shone through, guiding us, even when things felt overwhelmingly unclear.

We were thrust into a life that felt foreign, and though none of us were ready to let go of the past, acceptance became necessary for our healing.

We all shared the pain of loss, longing for the lives we once knew, but we found ourselves navigating uncharted waters.

For much of my life, I carried the weight of unhappiness.

My greatest aspiration became finding strength in my weakness because I discovered that one of the most beautiful aspects of serving God in our most trying moments is experiencing His strength when we feel we have none left.

"And he said unto me, my grace is sufficient for thee: for my strength is made perfect in weakness. Most gladly therefore will I rather glory in my infirmities, that the power of Christ may rest upon me." (2 Corinthians 12:9).

I write this book with the heartfelt intention to encourage those who find themselves in similar situations.

This scripture reassures me that even in my deepest pain, God is present, offering comfort and strength, showing that our service to Him is not diminished by our suffering.

Serving God during spells of depression often necessitates a significant shift in perspective for His strength is most evident in our weakness.

Rather than aiming to serve from my limited capacity, I have learned to embrace my vulnerability, inviting God's grace to carry me through my darkest moments.

In even the smallest acts of faith, I found profound expressions of obedience.

These gestures demonstrate a deep-rooted trust in God's ability to work miracles, even when I feel utterly depleted.

The journey of serving God while wrestling with depression is not one meant to be undertaken in isolation.

Even when words fail to express my turmoil, I find solace in the knowledge that the Holy Spirit intercedes on my behalf.

"Likewise, the Spirit also help our infirmities: for we know not what we should pray for as we ought: but the Spirit itself make intercession for us with groaning which cannot be uttered." (Romans 8:26).

I hold steadfast in the belief that God is always at work, even amid struggles, orchestrating everything for His glory and our ultimate good.

By leaning on the support of others, taking one deliberate step at a time, and drawing strength from my faith, I find reassurance in the truth that the road to recovery may indeed be long.

However, each victory, no matter how small, serves as a precious reminder that life's greatest treasures can never be taken away from us.

Chapter 12

Come unto me, all ye that labour and are heavy laden, and I will give you rest. Take my yoke upon you and learn of me; for I am meek and lowly in heart: and ye shall find rest unto your souls. For my yoke is easy, and my burden is light." (Matthew 11: 28-30).

Looking back, my experience in my abusive marriage was one of the hardest trials my children and I faced.

Yet, through it all, I discovered that even the darkest moments of our lives we can be transformed by God's grace and love for His glory.

Amidst the challenges of life, my mother was a beacon of hope, always urging us to hold on to our faith in the Lord.

As a prayer leader and a devoted believer, she exemplified the power of prayer, bringing her struggles before God with honesty and seeking support from church leaders.

Her resilience inspired us, reminding us that we are never truly alone.

In moments when I felt empty, God's power worked through me in ways I could never have imagined. Even amid our brokenness, my mother's prayers kept us anchored, allowing God's love to shine through as a vessel of hope.

Please, don't stop praying. Whatever life is throwing your way, cling to the Lord. Have hope and remember that we serve a God who is already intervening on our behalf, even when we can't see the result.

Faith in God is profoundly significant in our lives. As Psalm 68:5 beautifully states, He is "a father of the fatherless and a judge of the widows."

As a single parent, I faced countless obstacles while trying to create a better future for my children.

There were times when it felt overwhelmingly difficult to make ends meet, but through perseverance and faith, I witnessed remarkable changes in our lives.

My children, against all odds, progressed in their education and now hold impressive degrees and fulfilling jobs.

Life rarely resembles the perfect dream we envision; instead, it has unfolded in ways I never anticipated, ultimately leading to a beautiful existence.

Now, in my 70s, I continue to serve God with gratitude and dedication. Reflecting on my journey, it's clear that it was fraught with hurdles, setbacks, and moments of deep pain that tested my resolve at every turn.

Yet, amid these challenges, I discovered a profound truth that sustained me: no matter how imperfect or difficult life may seem, I never lost faith in God.

There were moments when my faith was pushed to its limit, particularly during times when the struggles bore down heavily on my family.

I would lie awake at night, my mind racing with worries about how I could provide for my children and ease their burdens.

In those dark nights of doubt, I felt as though I was failing, but I cling tightly to God, drawing strength from His presence.

I reminded myself repeatedly that His plans far exceed my own understanding, even when circumstances appeared chaotic and unjust.

Every relationship comes with its own unique share of struggles and trials. My marriage, which I regarded as a blessing, was not without its difficulties.

In moments of conflict and despair, I sought solace in prayer, earnestly asking God to heal the wounds that existed in our hearts.

Through this experience, I learned that even amidst imperfect relationships, God is capable of performing miracles if we are willing to surrender our worries to Him.

Although I sometimes felt inadequate and my patience wore thin, it was in those moments that God gently reminded me of His grace.

His grace is sufficient, and His strength is made perfect in our weaknesses. God never required me to be flawless; He simply asked for my trust.

Looking back on my life, I can now see how God was continually at work in every situation.

He transformed my struggles into lessons of perseverance, molding me into a more compassionate person towards others who are suffering.

Life remains far from perfect, and God does not promise us a life devoid of trials. However, He does assure us of His constant presence, walking beside us through every hardship we face.

He offers us strength during our weakest moments, hope when everything seems hopeless, and a peace that transcends understanding.

If you find yourself in a season of struggle, I urge you to not give up on God, for He has not given up on you.

Hold onto Him tightly, especially when life feels insurmountable. Trust that He is orchestrating everything for your good, even when it is difficult to see.

Faith is not about achieving perfection in life; it is fundamentally about trusting in God's unwavering goodness, even amidst life's most profound challenges.

Through it all, I am proud to say that three of my children successfully graduated from college. My oldest son, Roy, dedicated 28 years to work at one of the most prestigious university.

Each of my children has settled into loving marriages, blessing me with the joy of watching them raise their own families.

Life has taken an incredible turn for the better, and I am immensely grateful to witness the lives of my grandchildren unfold.

As Psalm 23:6 beautifully states, "Surely goodness and mercy shall follow me all the days of my life; and I will dwell in the house of the Lord forever."

If you are facing similar challenges, I want to encourage you with the assurance that God will never forsake you.

As Psalm 37:25 expresses, "I have been young, and now am old; yet have I not seen the righteous forsaken, nor his seed begging bread."

God is indeed a way maker, a problem solver, and a burden bearer.

Life is inherently unpredictable, often characterized by both triumphs and trials. For many, the imperfections of life and the strain of broken relationships can breed moments of doubt and despair.

In John 16:33, Jesus reassures us: "These things I have spoken unto you, that in me ye might have peace. In the world ye shall have tribulation: but be of good cheer; I have overcome the world."

Every struggle presents an opportunity to deepen our faith and testify of God's goodness.

Trials challenge the strength of our trust in God and create space for significant spiritual growth.

James 1:3-4 reminds us, "Knowing this, that the trying of our faith worketh patience. But let patience have her perfect work, that ye may be perfect and entire, lacking nothing."

While life's imperfections may tempt us to abandon our faith, these are the very moments when we most need to draw closer to God.

Through prayer, we can discover the strength to endure and allow our faith to blossom.

Philippians 4:6-7 encourages us not to be anxious, but to present our requests to God through prayer, assuring us that His peace will guard our hearts and minds.

Deuteronomy 31:6 powerfully states, "The Lord our God goes with you; He will never leave you nor forsake you."

Indeed, God remains faithful, even when life appears unfair or unbearable.

Ultimately, we must remember that our real hope lies not in the present but in God's eternal promises.

Life on earth will always be flawed because we inhabit a fallen world.

Nevertheless, Revelation 21:4 brings us comfort: "And God shall wipe away all tears from their eyes; and there shall be no more death, neither sorrow, nor crying, neither shall there be any more pain: for the former things are passed away."

To everyone reading this book, I want to offer support: Hold on tightly to Jesus. He is your provider, protector, healer, source of strength, comforter, and guide. In times of trouble, He will be your very-present help (Psalm 46:1).

Do not lose heart; trust in God wholeheartedly for He is indeed capable of seeing you through every trial.

No matter the size of your challenges, whether monumental or minor, God will lead you through.

As Zechariah 4:6 beautifully declares, "Not by might, nor by power, but by my spirit, saith the Lord of hosts."

It is often through our struggles that we draw closer to God and develop a deeper understanding of His grace.

My story is one of unwavering faith in hardship, and I hope it inspires others to seek solace in God during their own struggles.

I want to extend my encouragement to anyone going through tough times—please hold on and don't give up on God.

Even in your darkest hours, hope for healing and strength exists. Life can be incredibly challenging, but it is also an opportunity for resilience. Remember, your circumstances do not define your future.

Reflect on the qualities and abilities that make you unique; for no one can take them away from you.

A sense of purpose can provide you with something positive to strive towards.

I urge you to find joy even amidst difficulties, and don't hesitate to reach out to someone who can help.

Sharing your struggles can bring about the support you may need. Life is a testament of God's strength, and while each journey is unique, it can inspire hope in others.

God equips us with the tools to cope with life's challenges, and He intervenes to give us the strength and love we need to overcome.

As we navigate the rocky road of life, we remember that our existence holds purpose and value.

The trials we face today will lay the groundwork for a hopeful tomorrow. Keep holding on; brighter days are indeed on the horizon.

Made in United States
North Haven, CT
19 February 2025